Many Thi

Natural Poetry

by

People Living in Nursing Homes

Collection and Comment

by

Thomas E. Heinzen, Ph.D.

SEABURN

NEW YORK

ISBN: 1-885778-14-7

96 97 98 7 6 5 4 3 2

Library of Congress Cataloging-in-Publication Data

Many Things to Tell You: Natural Poetry/
edited by Tyra Onwuchekwa

Cover design © CSO, NY
Cover Photo © Peter Figetakis
Typesetting & Layout, M&K, PO Box 1114, New York, NY 10037

Printed in Canada
Seaburn Publishing offers books and cassettes. For more information write to Seaburn Publishing, PO Box 2085, LIC, New York 11102.

Contents

Contents Contd...

Contents Contd...

Contents Contd...

Contents Contd...

Acknowledgments

The first acknowledgment is to the contributors themselves, but the presentation of their creativity would not have happened without some very practical support. Senior Life Management provided the combination of clinical guidance and organizational discipline which allowed me to create a therapeutic environment that supported the achievements demonstrated in this book. The American Psychological Association also provided me with a useful discussion of the ethical issues related to respecting the rights of people living in nursing homes as we sought to publish their creativity. Colleagues at our Institute for Creative Aging at Wm. Paterson State College of New Jersey also provided strategic support and encouragement. At a far more personal level I am indebted to Joy Williams Brown, to the nursing homes themselves and to Mary Paoloni and Tom Pileggi for their guidance and support — of the residents first of all, and then of my efforts on their behalf.

An Introduction to Some Natural Poets

Many people living in nursing homes are accidental poets. Like most poets they are virtually unrecognized, unread, and unappreciated — even by themselves. But that lack of self-consciousness may be the very thing that makes people who live in nursing homes such magnificent poets. "Doctor," inquired one resident, leaning forward on her walker as I was politely trying to leave at the end of the day, "When you came to see me, was I there?" It was a reasonable question — but also startling, precise, provocative, spontaneous, tragic, full of double meanings, and just a little bit humorous. Like a great deal of "real" poetry it was a rich, insightful accident of speech that made me stop and think things over one more time.

People living in nursing homes use words for many creative purposes: to get rid of an undesired roommate, to persuade the dietician to serve more chocolate pudding, to distract themselves from disappointment, to drag humor into their difficult circumstances, and to ferry an enjoyable past into a painful present. They are creative at keeping wanderers out of their rooms, creative at manipulating relationships to their personal advantage, and creative at disguising embarrassing disabilities.

But their smoothest creativity, to me, evolves almost undetected. It is like the ocean tides quietly filling the upriver backwaters of the Hudson River with nutrients and wildlife. By listening carefully to the words these residents speak we can hear the gentle rise and fall of small but meaningful preferences, the push and pull of their everyday frustrations, the inlet and the outflow of their remaining dreams. This book reveals the natural inclination of very old people for poetic speech.

Spoken words are the water that people living in nursing homes have used to shape, polish and wear away at the rock of each others' complex personalities for more than eighty, ninety or even one hundred years. Speech is often the only way to initiate action in a nursing home, and even that form of action may be limited by stroke, Alzheimer's Disease, or some other unwelcome dysfunction that makes their words drip or leak to an unintended purpose. Consequently people living in nursing homes have grown accustomed to making their words matter.

For some, including those whose words you will read in this book, every breath represents significant physical effort; speech is not to be wasted. Like water, many of us use words carelessly and with little appreciation for their power to shape mountains, feed pastures, and grow tomatoes. Yet words are how most of us negotiate the important details of our lives. This is especially true of older people living in nursing homes who have become skilled at the use of words after eight or nine decades of daily practice.

The residents' own words, when read back to them or presented to them in a picture frame, are received with surprise and satisfaction. Even when memory function has not permitted recognition of their own words, these natural poets frequently respond with vigorous approval, grateful that someone else finally sees the world just the way they see it. Sometimes residents will even disagree with their own words, and offer editorial comment, dispassionate critique, and clarifying elaboration. We who are more self-conscious of our reputations would find it very difficult to offer such candid self-criticism.

The content of this book represents the many faceted experience of living in a nursing home, and overturns most of the negative stereotypes I once held regarding nursing home residents. Yes, there is dementia and depression and drooling and many sided desperation. But circulating amidst those troubles is a resilient and highly creative life force, even when expressed in the pursuit of a dignified death. Previous to this book, there has been almost no record of what life is like in a nursing home from the residents' perspective. Indeed, even in my own mind it is unclear whether these accounts are best described as poetry, oral history, or psychotherapy. So even though the content of this book lacks the controls necessary for a more trustworthy and generalizable research study, it does offer an observational starting point for understanding the nursing home experience.

Most of the poems collected in this book are the result of three years of psychotherapy practiced in two nursing homes in Queens, New York. Many of the contributors have been my patients (although much of my work encourages them to be anything but "patient"). Other contributions are from pleasant acquaintances I made while visiting. All have become good friends.

Each contributor, and in some cases a responsible family member as well, has given permission for their words to be published. I have grouped their poems and reflections into different content categories based on the major theme expressed in each account. Consequently, we have before us an organized collection of what people living in nursing homes are thinking about.

These categories are like islands of coherence emerging out of the deep confusion of nursing home life. The first category is a skill I had fancied I was good at: *Learning to Listen*. Then I offer a group of poems whose theme is intended to startle you, as it startled me when I finally was able to give it a name: *Beauty*. This section is followed by remarkably candid discussions of *Death and Dying*, a topic with distinct ethical and political overtones regarding the desire and the right to die. The consideration of death and dying leads many residents to reconsider their feelings and ideas about *God and Religion*. Residents also expressed *Personal Philosophies*, often inadvertently, as they attempted to describe the way their lives have worked. A curious topic developed over time, although I did not notice it very quickly: *Small Pleasures* describes what and how these residents continue to enjoy their lives. Why should I have been surprised that they enjoyed talking about pleasure? A significant number of poems reveal a century's worth of *Social History* followed by poems which represent the emotional seeds that grew into the movement we call *Feminism*. A significant number of poems also focus on the here and now of *Nursing Home Life*. Poems about *Anger and Depression* probably are not surprising to most observers of nursing home life, but the clarity with which these experiences is conveyed is painfully vivid. Some of the most beautiful and anguished memories expressed by these residents focus on *Marriage and Families*. A more unexpected theme was the expression of *Curiosity*, followed by some general reflections about *Aging*. Many of these poems bubble with a quiet but compelling humor — both intended and accidental. Humor doesn't have its own section so you'll simply have to "get it" whenever it floats by. There are other ways to organize this collection, but this seemed to best serve the purpose of understanding the experience of nursing home life.

The act of publishing this book is intended to be therapeutic for the contributors and their families — a source of pride, a recognition of psychological worth, and a permanent record of lives well lived. But the publishing of this book aims at a larger social purpose. It demonstrates that people living in nursing homes do not deserve to be stereotyped, either positively or negatively. People living in nursing homes are neither "old and wise" nor "completely ga-ga." The people represented in this book deserve praise because they display individuality and variety despite living in a fiercely institutional environment. They demonstrate creativity in the midst of suffering, use humor as a defense against everyday frustration, and search for meaning while living in wrenching circumstances. But these same courageous people also display selfishness, short temper, unreasonableness, life-long habits of manipulation and just plain bad manners. Much of the unappealing behavior within a nursing home is a simple, poorly expressed cry to be treated as an individual. It may sound like a chant, a shriek or nagging but the words within the words are often very simple to translate: Pay attention to me!

Not surprisingly, several of the contributors represented in this book have died. You will get to know some of the individuals represented in this book very well, as they slowly reveal themselves to you in different sections. Others (or their families) hid behind the author known as Anonymous. Touching these lives is akin to watching the last five minutes of a gripping movie: I can only surmise what the plot must have been to produce the endings that they share with me. It is a particular pleasure for me to offer you, the reader, these words as a potential influence in the unfolding plot of your own life.

Fly Fishing for Poetry in a Nursing Home

A Dedication

My father has been trying to teach me how to fly fish for more than forty years. The lessons "took" very nicely for my brother who can stare at a stream and seemingly mesmerize trout to the end of his leader. And his son, my nephew, seems to have an extra measure of the useless gift, despite living in Brooklyn. Fortunately, just enough of what my father was trying to teach me did hook my attention so that his lessons reappeared when I began to practice the art of psychology among people living in nursing homes. I began to notice small "rises" of beauty when residents would speak, small "fishy" looking patches when residents would show extra coyness, and heart stopping excitement when a group of residents would start hatching glorious poems faster than I could write them down. As I worked at this skill, it began to feel more and more like the kind of fishing my father had been trying to teach me, but with the gratifying twist that these fish really wanted to be caught. So maybe some of my parents' lessons, delivered in their own peculiar ways, continue to benefit me at a level beyond that which any of us can clearly understand. I am glad to dedicate the "trophy poems" in this collection to my parents, Bruce and Clare, with gratitude for those many (but still too few) hours spent quietly listening and watching the flow of life on a trout stream.

Learning to Listen

Think of the different kinds of listening required by each of the following professions: Physicians and poets, composers and psychotherapists, actors and critics. Each is trained to listen, assess, and act based on what they have heard. The quality of listening required to serve people living in a nursing home requires a blend of all these listening styles. It requires listening for both symptoms of illness and expressiveness of affect, for the music in their voices and the words they leave unsaid, for their public and private performances and how they view their own behavior.

Such a "job" is far too complex, for me or for anyone. Fortunately, the simple act of paying attention is therapeutic, all by itself, even when that attention misses so many relevant details. Paying attention to people who live in nursing homes means far more than cataloging their psychological score on a Mini-Mental Status Exam or a Depression Inventory. Notice, in the following poems, how earnestly these residents express their need to be listened to by someone who believes in their creativity.

The poem "Many Things to Tell You" expresses the mental plight of many people living in nursing homes. The author knows his memory will work, if only someone will stimulate his thinking with careful listening. When I was greeted with the words in "Please Don't Mind" I barely noticed that the author had told me something wonderful about herself. In spite of her struggle to remember and to communicate clearly she was telling me, with heroic courtesy, that she knew she did not always make sense, and she wanted me to know that she knew that, and to ask for my understanding and patience as a listener. But I came terribly close to missing that poignantly expressed plea for understanding. It would have been so easy simply to label her as "Confused." (In fact, paying attention to cognitive deficits, what people cannot do, is the focus of a great deal of psychological testing and clinical training.) But that label would do this author a serious injustice.

An observer might believe that such a label would be easy to apply to Edith Mulligan ("Please"). Her loss of motor control has affected both her limbs and her speech — but not her desire to be paid attention to. Nor have those disabilities affected her psychological ability to assert herself, in the loudest and longest whisper she could sustain as I supplied her with morning coffee. Edith Carr and Esther Carroll, on the other hand, were beautifully lucid in the way they instructed me in what to listen for, as I worked within their nursing home. They gave me my job description.

Many Things to Tell You
Anonymous
(b. 1900; composed 1995)

Please...don't let time pass
Until you come again
Because I have many things to tell you
That I don't remember.

Please Don't Mind
Anonymous
(b. 1918; composed 1995)

Please don't mind
If sometimes
I don't understand
What I'm saying.

Please
by Edith Mulligan
(b. 1907; composed 1996)

Please.
Look at my eyes.
Thank you.

Your Job
by Edith Carr
(b. 1911; composed 1995)

Your job is to remind people
Of beautiful moments
They didn't know they had.

Some Silly Little Thing
by Esther Carroll
(b. 1911; composed 1995)

There's people here,
Two of 'em,
Over a hundred.

I used to think,
"You live that long,
You must know something."

But I found out
It's only common incidents
That they remember.

Something in their childhood
When they were little:
Some silly little thing.

Beauty

The presence of beauty is not what comes to mind when one thinks of a nursing home. Nevertheless, beauty survives, secreted away in memory until its release into awareness is triggered by some memory cue. Even so, residents seldom had a sense that they had expressed anything profound or beautiful until I pointed it out to them — then they agreed with sincere enthusiasm! Sarah Fitzgerald, for example, speaks with a haiku-like quality, becoming more fluent with every productive exchange. But she stubbornly yielded up the name of each flower, literally word by word, when she first composed "That's Wild Beauty." First, I asked her if there were flowers in her native Ireland. She answered me "Yes," and we sat quietly together for several long moments until I finally asked her "What Kind?" and she informed me that it depended. Eventually I asked her for the details, which she provided, but only when I prompted her repeatedly after each flower was named by saying "Anything else?" The second verse of her poem was elicited with equal effort after I asked her if she had enjoyed the flowers. "Yes," she said, "Nice to look at." She issued her final line as a way of ending our conversation and dismissing me until the following week. Yet what emerged was as beautiful as the flowers she remembered!

Making residents aware of their potential to express something beautiful proved to be a very satisfying exchange for them. Dorothy Dade offered her elegant final two lines only after I had offered my genuine admiration for her previous expressions. Lillian Claus' aside about the sound of Spanish on her Germanic ear was almost too quicksilver for me to catch, but she beamed with pleasure when I pointed out what a beautifully turned phrase she had used. Emmanuel Woodson, on the other hand, knew he had a good story to tell and he enjoyed telling it with style, grateful for an audience he could twist around his finger. The beauty in their words had been sitting there, ready to be expressed, needing only the encouragement of a believer in their creativity.

Perhaps the most poignant of these expressions is the reflection offered by Anna Becker. She had not spoken more than two words to me over a fairly long period of time, appearing to fit the worst stereotype of a forlorn nursing home resident. Normally I would crouch by her wheel chair so she could look down on me as I touched her hands and endeavored to stimulate some kind of response. After a number of weeks, she spoke these words, not in a rush, but all together as a finished product, looking steadily at me before she returned to her habitual posture.

That's Wild Beauty
by Sarah Fitzgerald
(b. 1926; composed 1995)

Yes, there were flowers in Ireland —
Depends on where you are:
Wild flowers, buttercups, daisies,
Clover, primroses, daffodils.

Nice to look at.
Nice to smell.
Nice to leave just where they are:
In the fields in Ireland.

The Flirtation Waltz
by Dorothy Dade
(b. 1911; composed 1995)

I enjoyed the Flirtation Waltz
More than all the other dances.
I danced with my husband;
I was better than he was.
He knew that.
Everybody knew that.

It's hard to say what it felt like:
I felt so relaxed.
I used to flirt with my husband
When we were dancing (it was part of the dance).
And the audience would applaud.
Ohhhh...yes! They would applaud.

You think this poem is beautiful?
You should have seen us when we danced!

The Language is Liquid
by Lillian Claus
(b. 1900, composed 1995)

I just came back from Spain
And I wished I knew the language better,
Because the language is liquid:
It just flows out of them.

A Pretty Day
by Emmanuel Woodson
(b. 1917; composed 1995)

When I see a sunny day like this
I feel like it's going to be another good day!
When the sun is coming up, the jaybird says:
"Youcanmakeit!Youcanmakeit!Youcanmakeit!"
Then a snowbird flies by and says:
"Awwwww, sheeeeit!"

I Could Make Anyone Look Good!
by Dorothy Dade
(b. 1911; composed 1995)

I was a teenager when I started dancing:
  A young teenager.
My Uncle used to dance with me and my two oldest brothers:
  I was quite young.

I was easy to teach — It just came natural to me
  (And my Uncle could dance well.)
As a young girl dancing with my Uncle, I felt important.
  Grown up, almost.

I could dance with my father, too,
  But I would dance with anybody who could dance.
Sometimes I would make up dances with my Uncle.
  It felt nice when I invented something —

Like I knew what I was doing.
  And I did, too.
My feet could follow anybody — make a bad dancer look good.
  But I didn't like to.

I've been sick and my feet are slower
  Than they used to be.
I could do any kind of dancing, but now I don't think about it
  Unless somebody says something.

I hate to say it, but it's true.
  Everybody used to say it:
"Dorothy Dade could make anyone
  Look good!"

A Dream That I Lived
by Margaret Ray
(b. 1903; composed 1995)

I always dream about something in Ireland.
I don't seem to dream about anything here.

I dream about doing work in Ireland:
Taking care of cows, sheep, and oh yes! plenty of chickens.

The work made me feel good:
Taking care of things.

It's not hard work in my dream.
I didn't feel it was hard work when I did it, either.

To me,
Ireland is a dream that I lived.

Times Come and Times Pass
by Anna Becker
(b. 1901, composed 1995)

Times come and times pass.

There are little stretches
Which are beautiful,
And times when
You lose hope for the better.

Death and Dying

Death is very close in a nursing home. Once I observed a harried funeral director insist on trying to take a recently dead resident out through the crowded day room in order to avoid the more discreet but difficult to manage back steps of the nursing home. It required the combined efforts of the Director of Nursing and others to prevent this crude intrusion. Some nursing home residents have indicated that the chief restraint to their desire for suicide is the social stigma it would leave behind for their loved ones. For others, the only force that stays their hand is the inability to lift their hand — and a bit of knowledge. Steve Galligan's statistical assertion at the end of "The Danger Line" may or may not be true. But the feelings that give "life" to the idea of dying are omnipresent.

Nevertheless, nursing homes are not hospices; they serve the living, not the "just about to die." True, most residents live near the edge, some are rapidly approaching the edge, a few are taking very long walks alongside the edge — and they are quite naturally thinking, feeling and wondering a great deal about death and dying. Consequently, the closeness of death permeates the details of everyday living: their willingness to form friendships, the certainty of their religious beliefs, their attitudes towards pain and medication, and their anxiety reactions when an accustomed face is not in its usual place. Perhaps because of the nearness of death most residents express, not horror, but a combination of humor and reconciliation (both with and without the support of a religious faith) as they consider death and the dying process that gets them there.

The author of "That's a Savings" expresses no interest in religion, but is most concerned with not being a burden to those he leaves behind, who have been so generous with him. For him, dying cheap is part of living well. Depression shows up too, but as a part of living soon to be dispensed with rather than as a part of death and dying. Often, death and dying are considered through the mist of dementia and reduced verbal processing. I find that such "deficits" do not diminish but enhance the quality of their words. Like our highly selective memories of childhood, we sometimes retain only what is peculiarly most important, the deeper grooves in our thought patterns, as we anticipate the end of our natural lives.

In these words about death and dying I also find humor, beauty and despair sitting literally side by side, wheelchair by wheelchair. Esther Carroll still feels the jazz while George Socrates looks for a way out and Polonia Rios searches for a way to wait. She articulates the cry of so many in pain, in her case with a crippling rheumatoid arthritis, waiting with a remarkably sturdy faith in the face of deep confusion. Another anonymous contributor articulates a far more common attitude towards Death in "Mostly I Leave It Alone," displaying both style and humor. Neither dying nor death sounds very frightening to Bertha Hickey in "I Want to Go Like Elsie." Dying sounds beautiful. Perhaps it is.

It is psychologically interesting to note what is absent from these poems about death and dying. There is an anxiety to die soon clearly expressed in "If There Were a Way" and "How Do I Get That?" but no fear of death. There is despair about living in pain, but no fear that death itself will disappoint them. The idea of death is so familiar that it takes on a new meaning. As suggested in "How Do I Get That?" death is the desired friend, dying the nuisance companion.

How Do I Get That?
Anonymous
(b. 1910; composed 1996)

If I stop breathing,
I die.
Right?

How do I get that?

If There Were a Way
by George Socrates
(b. 1906; composed 1996)

If there were
A way of dying
Without any difficulty
I would do it.

The Danger Line
by Steve Galligan
(b. 1902; composed 1996)

I only have a quarter of one lung left
So it wouldn't take much to knock me off.

If I get pneumonia,
That puts me right on the Danger Line.

The only thing you hope is
When it happens you go quick.

It's a terrible thing to gasp for breath
When you're dying.

I don't want to live on the Danger Line.
They brought me back twice and I don't know why.

Twice I was green —
Right on the Danger Line.

The woman next to me said "I saved your life."
And I said "Thanks for nothing."

I hope the next time I'm on the Danger Line
I tip the other way

And I bet you 9/10 of the people here
Would say the same thing.

I Want to Go Like Elsie
by Bertha Hickey
(b. 1924; composed 1996)

Ahh... Listen to that music:
They're bringing back all the old songs.

Ohh... "Moonlight in Vermont":
I like this...nice...

When I exit this life...like in Cabaret:
I want to go like Elsie.

Mostly I Leave It Alone
Anonymous

I think about dying every day
But I really don't know much about it.
Mostly I leave it alone
And hope I go quick.

That's a Savings
by Steve Galligan
(b. 1902; composed 1996)

I called the funeral home,
I said: "Please, no prayers...
And the same clothes I'm wearing now."

I said: "Give me an estimate.
I want a very cheap job."
What am I going to get out of a fancy funeral?

I said: "A plain white casket,
Or a pine casket —
Whatever's cheapest."

I'm thinking: "There's the pickup costs,
The casket costs and the funeral costs."
What else is there?

I don't believe in religion.
That's a savings!
Just an American flag on me as I go.

I bet I die before June.
I'll miss Belmont Park.
That's the only thing.

Plus Fifty Cents for Shipping and Handling
by Esther Carroll
(b. 1911; composed 1995)

In New Orleans they walk on down behind the hearse:
Glassed in and full of flowers!
We followed, my brother and I,
And all the traffic came to a stop.

We heard the music and followed,
But only as far as we dared:
To the graveyard at the Elysian Fields
Right at the end of Rampart Street.

They invented jazz down in New Orleans.
That jazz!
Your feet, your hands:
Everything wants to move!

When I die I just want to be cremated.
I'm already paid up on that:
Fifteen hundred dollars to be cremated
Plus fifty cents for shipping and handling!

When I cremated my husband,
Twenty-five years ago, it was only $750.00.
The ship's name is the New York Exchange Ship —
I wonder who they're going to exchange for me?

I Only Can Wait for God
by Polonia Rios
(b. 1903; composed 1995)

The pain is too much.
The pain is all in my hands.
The medicine does nothing for me.
When you touch my fingernails, it hurts.

I don't think I'm ready to die.
I said that at first, I was,
But I changed my mind.

Please don't touch me.

I say to God
"Tonight?
When I go to sleep,
I will die for you tonight."

And then I wake up
And God has not taken me.
I don't understand.

I only can wait for God.

I'll Let You Know
Anonymous

Hey! You hit my leg!
Don't worry, I'm OK.
When I'm dead,
I'll let you know.

God and Religion

As we age, it seems only natural to review the quality of our lives in light of some higher or more permanent standard of evaluation than we may have used in our busier, more ambitious years. Although God and religion appear throughout this collection, I have chosen the poems in this section because they seem to represent common but underlying beliefs. For example, the quality of faith which inspired Anna Schneider's first two poems ("I Guess God Must Love Me" and "God Forgot Me") probably represents the more subtle "faith response" many of us display in response to our circumstances: good events mean God loves us; bad events mean God forgot us. Out of this quiet theological confusion emerges the reality described by Anna Schneider's third poem: "Who Really Knows?"

Religion still wields a two-edged sword among nursing home residents, dividing between God and the human institutions which promote religious activity. I sense the momentum of character in Andreas Constantinou, a Brother in the Greek Orthodox Church. His words in "Manners" reflect the difficult challenge of daily service to God and the sometimes ill-mannered people God created. He can't stop caring and the authenticity of his faith comes sounding through his memory difficulties in "The Resurrection."

On the other hand, the failures of religious institutions are felt just as deeply sixty and seventy years after the events, as testified to by the authors of "Fear and Love," "How We Became Lutherans" and "Tell Me What You Really Think!" There is a quiet but remarkable statement embedded in Delia Looney's poem when she self observes that "It's only lately that I'm beginning to think for myself." People living in nursing homes do not stop re-thinking, self-examining, or searching for meaning. For some, the two-edged sword becomes sharper than ever.

The desperate nursing home situation helps both to reveal and to shape what residents believe. Think of the compel-

ling forces testing their faith: impending death, declining function, physical pain, unpleasant peers, failures in the family, an
imperfect staff, and extreme loss of personal control. The nursing home situation ruthlessly "peels" away layers of social pres-
tige, reputation, self-image — even the protective influence of
money and daily habits.

None of us really knows how we will react or what we
will believe until we find ourselves in the actual situation. Rose
Milana's stark description of family loss leads to an even starker
description of what proved to be a temporary faith loss. Madeline
Vermilya sighs deeply — and turns, as ever, to God. Sarah
Fitzgerald expresses the everyday experience of many others in
the title of her poem ("One Can Doubt But Still Believe") and in
the logic by which she comes to that conclusion. Yet some expressions of faith are so natural that they seem to be the product
of some deep insight or secret knowledge, as in "The End of the
Rainbow." It is not an overtly religious expression — yet it is
candidly the most faith filled statement I have ever heard. The
nursing home situation is helping these residents to discover the
depths of their own faith!

I Guess God Must Love Me
by Anna Schneider
(b. 1904; composed 1995)

Look! New dentures!
And they don't jump around!
And they were free of charge!

And a new blanket from a girlfriend!
I just got it last night!
It all happened last night!

And my nails!
They got painted red!
They're beautiful!

New nails!
No charge for the dentures!
A brand new blanket!

I used to think
God didn't love me anymore.
But this week OK — we'll see about next week.

All this good news!
Somebody's going to have
A tear in the eye!

God Forgot Me
by Anna Schneider
(b. 1904; composed 1995)

We're glad we did it:
We traveled.
We had a wonderful time
When we were young.

I can't remember
All the cities,
All the countries:
There were so many different ones.

Switzerland, Austria,
Germany, partially Poland,
Yugoslavia, Slovenia —
I can't remember them all.

All the pictures...
When we go,
They will all go
In the garbage.

God forgot me.

Who Really Knows?
by Anna Schneider
(b. 1904; composed 1996)

I want to die
But I don't die
And I wonder why?

God must be scared of me.

That's not really true,
And I'm not scared of God
(But I don't make fun of Him either)

I guess God just doesn't want me yet.
Maybe there's too many people like me up there.
Who really knows?

Isn't That Enough?
by Rose Milana
(b. 1906; composed 1995)

My son-in-law died.
My sister died.
My brother died.
Someone else died,
But I can't think who.

My hope died,
A long time ago.
My faith died,
But only the first time.
But isn't that enough?

Yes, I Believe in My God
by Madeline Vermilya
(b. 1911; composed 1995)

I don't let things bother me.
If it's going to happen, it's going to happen.
I believe God's in control of everything
And He won't let anything bad happen to me.

I sit here and think and think and think.
I think about the family mostly.
I've got nothing else to do.

I think about years ago...
Growing up...

Ah...God help us.

One Can Doubt But Still Believe
by Sarah Fitzgerald
(b. 1926; composed 1996)

I just believe
The way I was brought up to believe:
Brought up to believe
In God.

It's not too complicated.

When bad things happen
They're never that bad.
When good things happen
I don't even try to explain it.

One can doubt but still believe.

They're so many people opposite
Who don't believe in God.
That's their own problem
And some of them pray anyway.

The Resurrection
by Andreas Constantinou
(b. 1907; composed 1995)

The Resurrection...
Well, people don't do it
Very often.

No, they don't.
And anything they do
Is very famous.

Tell Me What You Really Think!
Anonymous

I don't go to church.
It's not for me,
And I'll tell you why:

On the day my daughter was going to receive Communion
She slipped and had a little water.
You know, she was nervous and her mouth was dry.

She had the dress and the bouquet and everything
And then some gossip, a woman of course,
right in the neighborhood
Wouldn't let her receive because of the water.

We stopped everything right there
And I hope to God that woman —
I hope that woman got struck with something!

My Mother was strict: She stopped.
My husband was an altar boy: He stopped.
And I wouldn't let my kids go to the Catholic School.

Besides, I don't think there's a God anyway.
Do you really think there's a God?
Come on! Tell me what you really think!

Fear and Love
by Delia Looney
(b. 1902; composed 1996)

When the Mission people came
(The Priests from other churches)
The married women went the first week,
The married men were the second week,
And then the young people.

When they started preaching about having children,
The way he talked, it was as if we were all going to Hell!
"The women, the women, the women..."
He talked to us women about not spilling the seed!
Well, why didn't he tell that to the men?!

When I asked my husband when he got home "What did he say?"
He said, "Nothing. He talked religion."
But they scared me so bad the sweat just poured off of me!
I really felt Hell — we were so afraid of the Priests back then
And now I can't understand what makes Priests any different!

There used to be a lot of talk about Hell in those days:
The good people and the bad people,
The right hand and the left.
We were taught more Fear than Love
But I think God's more Love than Fear.

It's only lately that I'm beginning to think for myself.
Those old Priests were dreadful!
The young men learned more about sin in confessions
From the Priest asking questions
Than they ever figured out for themselves!

How We Became Lutherans
Anonymous

My Grandmother lived on the lower East side.
She went to the pier to cool off
On a hot summer night —
Fell asleep,
Fell off,
Drowned.

The Priest said she committed suicide
But it wasn't true.
So we all became Lutherans.

Me, I'm sort of a Catholic.

Manners
by Andreas Constantinou
(b. 1907; composed 1995)

Well...I tell you

When people go to church
You find out the difference
Between who and who.

Some are just wise guys.
They feel they are bigger than you
And they want to show off.

But if you are good to people,
You get the same.
Very few people have no manners.

It's the way they're brought up:
They think they are the best,
And you are nothing.

They have no manners:
They have to be given manners
By their parents.

As a priest
You have to have manners
Before you go to church.

You don't want to judge,
You want to love and let love.
Show people!

Just don't think you're bigger than anyone.
When you don't care about anyone else,
You're no good for the people.

The End of the Rainbow
Anonymous

I'm sure that
At the end of the rainbow
There's something I'm going to like
And stay liking it.

Personal Philosophy

Religious faith sometimes leads to confusion between what we are supposed to believe and what we really believe. So I find myself listening very closely for what these particular nursing home residents really believe. This is a very pleasant experience for me because I am genuinely interested. However, it requires tremendous alertness on my part since residents are likely to reveal some of these beliefs only when some little situation prompts them to reveal themselves, usually cloaked in humor or disguised in a casual comment (as George Socrates does in "But I Still Believe It").

For example, Elisa Pisani offered some of her personal philosophy ("Charge It!") during a rather ordinary discussion about the cost of yarn and my constant search for a better bargain. But she spilled something enlightening here, especially as someone who became part of the "credit card generation" only after she was raised with a very different set of values about money and debt. Helen Trcka also offered a bit of her private philosophy while we discussed the best way for her to manage the nursing home staff. I suspect that Helen's recognition that "Life is too short" inspires many others in the same way — they just lack Helen's candor! Anna Schoep's poem ("I Try to Pass on Happiness") demonstrates how the unpleasant features of the nursing home situation are especially helpful at revealing what residents really believe, whether or not it is what they are "supposed" to believe.

As Alice Mishkin's quiet observation makes clear, many people in nursing homes want to talk about how they have found meaning in life in the process of coping with the events of their lives — as well as how to cope with the events that life continues to throw at them. One of my frequent introductory questions when I meet a new resident is meant to be a bit humorous, and to inspire reflection. I ask them "Was your life easy?" (Usual answer: "No!") or "When did your life become easy?" (Usual answer: "Never!") or "Was your life more difficult than most other peoples' lives?" (Usual answer: "Yes!").

I hesitate to compare the lives of children with the lives of nursing home residents, but I have come to believe that children and nursing home residents are far more resilient than we give them credit for. Both Esther Carroll ("Half the battle Licked") and Florence Robertson ("A Very, Very Hard Life") reveal significant, life long resiliency as they review past coping styles and present courage. Esther Carrol goes even further into a search for truth, offering her own semi-serious ideas with the tantalizing suggestion that "Maybe the truth is somewhere in between all the theories."

Sometimes a particular coping strategy suggests a richer philosophy of life. It is interesting to speculate whether the personal philosophy expressed in "Make Believe" reveals how Brother Andreas managed conflicts within the monastery or a more general wisdom about how to survive relationships. Similarly, I have often needed the advice offered by George Socrates' review of his business life.

Two of the especially meaningful comments in this section come from individuals who have suffered substantial memory loss, implying organic brain insults related to aging. The author of "Crying Helps for the Heart" had instructed me in how to listen within the nursing home. Over time I came to recognize that she seemed best able to articulate her thoughts in couplets — she became disoriented beyond that point. But if I listened very carefully, I could learn what she was trying to say and support her in the effort. I found her last line to me especially intriguing: how does she know that? Where and how is that accurate information and insight registering in her brain? And what prompted her to say that?

Charge It!
by Elisa Pisani
(b. 1913; composed 1995)

Life:
I take it as it comes.
Then I charge it.

I don't know
Who I'm charging it to,
But I charge it!

Johnny Come Lately
by Helen Trcka
(b. 1914; composed 1995)

I have to complain and whine.
Why? Because life is too short.
Everything is too short and nothing goes right.
So I have to do all my complaining now!

But I Still Believe It
by George Socrates
(b. 1906; composed 1996)

So I lost my foot
And then my leg.

I believe
Everything works for the best.

It wasn't true in my case,
But I still believe it.

Half the Battle Licked
by Esther Carroll
(b. 1911; composed 1995)

No matter where you are
You got to take something,

So you may as well
Take what you got.

If you learn that,
You got half the battle licked!

A Very, Very Hard Life
by Florence Robertson
(b. 1906; composed 1995)

I had a very, very hard life.
I wish I knew what made it so hard?
I always just made the best of it.
But it was always very, very hard.

Make Believe
by Andreas Constantinou
(b. 1907; composed 1995)

Make believe
There's something wonderful
In the other person.

Decide
by George Socrates
(b. 1906; composed 1995)

Make decisions quickly.
You have to whether you like it or not.
If you can't sell in one place,
You have to move to another.

If you don't decide quickly
You find it financially difficult
And you waste time.
Sooner or later, you decide anyway.

Continuation of Existence
by Esther Carroll
(b. 1911; composed 1995)

I believe the liver and the lungs and all
Lived before we existed
And they came together
To make the body.

Then we advance the world,
Die and have a rest,
Come back where we're needed,
Maybe in a million years, maybe in ten million.

There was a time
When I didn't believe in anything.
Now I believe we're the Gods:
We make the world what it is.

We all have a theory —
That's mine.
And maybe the truth is somewhere
In between all the theories.

We're like a mushroom:
Parasites living off other things.
When I read all of this written down
I'll think that I was drunk!

We're something, though —
Just trying to figure out what!
Sometimes when there's no hope for anything
You see the most.

Crying Helps for the Heart
Anonymous

Crying helps for the heart,
But not to kill yourself.

The parents are always fast for the children,
But the children never go fast for the parents.

Crying doesn't help,
But what am I going to do?

It's easy to be nice,
But it's nice to be fresh.

When you're married it's different;
I can tell that you are married.

Other People's Lives
by Alice Mishkin
(b. 1911; composed 1995)

You have to see
Other people's lives
Before you recognize
Your own.

I Try to Pass on Happiness

by Anna Schoeps
(b. 1914; composed 1996)

I try to pass on happiness.

I had this beautiful scarf —
It had all different kinds of birds
All different colors
All around the border.

I knew someone would steal it
So I gave it away.

Small Pleasures

The experience of pleasure is stored in the brain much like a library stores books and a computer stores files. Like a library or a computer, the brain is subject to misfiling, theft, and computer viruses — problems which make the retrieval of information difficult and leading to the well known "tip of the tongue" phenomena: we know that we know but we can't quite produce the memory. It can be a very frustrating experience. Among the psychological material that nursing home residents have stored away for safe keeping are small pleasures, unintentionally remembered just because they were distinctive! Quite often residents cannot recall the event which contributed to such pleasure, but they retain a sense of enjoyment and are glad to relive it — if I can help them to discover the appropriate memory cue.

The anonymous author of "Just Kidding Around" is bursting with memory cues that make the memory of previous pleasures easy to retrieve. She cues herself — constantly. But for Irene Willett, the memory cue was more subtle: the word "Beer." Her face became animated, her voice more enthused, her entire affect became invigorated as she re-enjoyed past pleasures. She offered me those words early in the morning, on a cold day towards the end of a very long winter, before any warm weather was presenting itself with the hopeful cues of Spring and the coming Summer. The word "Beer," all by itself, cued a network of positive memories of hot weather, good food, and a Brooklyn brewery.

Food cues also worked well at producing re-enjoyment of chocolate cake, happy dilemmas (which should I eat first: the icing or the cake?), favorite recipes, and sage advice. When I protested to Stella Papa (just turned one hundred years old) that a recipe would make me fat, she countered with "Don't worry. Next week, I'll give you the thin recipe." For another resident, the cue is simply an oft repeated conversation that almost always produces enjoyment for her. "Thank you," I tell her with blind sincerity. She beams, and tells me "You're welcome — for what?" "Just for talking to me," I tell her, and she graciously responds "Oh, that! Think nothing of it." I am not sure what she is recalling, but it is pleasurable to her to feel listened to and appreciated, and this approach frequently leads to some very interesting recollections.

The act of remembering is pleasurable in itself, even when the content of the memory is painful. During Sarah Taub's remembered tennis pleasures, I raced back and forth from one end of her bedrail to the other, always returning the ball verbally back to her at center court until she glanced at my stomach halfway through the point. Remembered pleasures declare themselves again in Anna Caracciolo's humorous memory "The Red Jaw" and in how Sarah Fitzgerald recalls uniquely Irish enjoyments. These "frail" elderly enjoy mental stimulation the same a way a golfing addict can replay every stroke of a successful round; their mental pleasures are much like our own. Perhaps we would do well to think of a nursing home as a resource full of psychological pleasures, accidental wisdom, historic details, and humorous challenges — a lending library of sorts whose books may need sorting but never can be overdue.

Just Kidding Around
Anonymous

Hey, I'd like to be alone with you!
Come on in to my room.
Don't worry — I'm just kidding around.
I can't do nothing anymore anyhow.
Come to think of it —
The fun always was in the kidding around.

Brooklyn Beer
by Irene Willett
(b. 1917; composed 1996)

I love beer:
I used to drink Rheingold.
Oh, gosh! I loved beer!

On a hot day...
It was delicious —
On a cold day, too.

Could be for a sandwich.
Could be for anything.
I never liked getting drunk,

I just liked the beer.
Sometimes I drank it by myself,
Sometimes with friends.

A hot day
With a cold beer:
Delicious!

Easy to Have Fun in Brooklyn
by Edith Mulligan (b. 1907)
Irene Willett (b. 1917)
(composed 1996)

Prospect Park? That's far away.
The Brooklyn Bridge? A long trip.
Downstairs? That's a long way off.

I miss Brooklyn:
The ball games,
My old school,
The gang,
The boys,
The girls...

They're not far away.
They're pretty near,
And there's a nurse here —
She really reminds me of Brooklyn!

It was easy to have fun in Brooklyn.

Chocolate Cake
by Alice Mishkin
(b. 1911; composed 1995)

Oh, boy,
Does it taste good:
Chocolate cake!

The icing's the best part.
Of course, the cakes good, too.
I'm not really sure which is best.

If I had a nice piece of
Chocolate cake, chocolate icing,
Right here, right now,

I don't know what I'd do.
I'd eat the icing first,
Then I'd eat the cake.

Tennis...I Just Want to Play It
by Sarah Taub
(b. 1907; composed 1996)

It's a great game!
I don't know what it is about it
That makes it so good...

I like to make my opponents run!
It's good for them...
Takes a little bit off that tummy.

When I feel a racquet in my hand
I feel like a King
Especially when I am starting off.

When I hit the ball just right
And it goes where I want
I feel like...

I don't think about tennis now.
I just want to play it.

The Red Jaw
by Anna Caracciolo
(b. 1923; composed 1996)

One thing I didn't have was a boyfriend:
　I used to beat them up.
We used to have wars
　Down on Riverside Drive at 72nd St.:

You know that big hill going down to the park?
　It was the boys against the girls.
I'd punch them right in the face
　And they would run away.

They had one guy on the other side:
　A big bruiser of a guy.
One time he was standing behind a woman
　(The big coward).

Maybe he didn't want to fight.
　He was actually a nice guy —
But then he came across me:
　I punched him right in the jaw.

Whether I hurt him or not I don't know,
　But it was red —
I'll always remember that.
　But then he disappeared with his big, red jaw.

If I met him today
　I bet I wouldn't know him.
The swelling in his jaw
　Has probably gone down.

The Best Part of My Day is the Newspaper
by Jane Hodik
(b. 1901; composed 1996)

I'm having pains around my heart.
I can hardly see out of my one good eye.
My body feels weak.
Aches everywhere.

I think old age has a lot to do with it.
I'm ninety-five — that's pretty old.
My emotions aren't too good either.
I spend most of my time in my room.

There's not one thing
That makes me feel good,
But I just make the best of everything.
The best part of my day is the newspaper.

For Enjoyment, In Ireland
by Sarah Fitzgerald
(b. 1926; composed 1996)

In Ireland
You don't have a lot of friends:
You're too busy.

In Ireland
Very few people go to pubs:
Very few people can afford it.

For enjoyment in Ireland
We sit in front of a fire
Singing and telling stories.

In front of the hot stone
We tell graveyard stories
And stories that don't exist.

My grandmother told one
About a boy in a graveyard
Who said:

"Don't take that one — That's my Uncle.
Don't take that one — It's my Grandmother.
Don't take that one — It's some relative."

That's what we did for enjoyment.

Social History

Included in this section are poems and memories which somehow comment on historical events, both famous and trivial. The interweaving of the famous and the mundane creates a startling verbal fabric. For example, I think you will agree that Inez Johnson's description of "Benny's Favorite Shoes" represents a small but colorful thread in jazz history. In this section we visit the odd combinations of people, places, and events that make working with this population so uniquely satisfying.

A serious problem and an intellectual delight of working with this immigrant oriented population is the multiplicity of native languages: eight at one 200 bed facility! It is poignantly unkind not to have a native speaker on staff: how does one ask for toileting assistance, register a complaint, ask for a shade to be drawn, or enjoy television? If the staff, too, converses in an unknown tongue, it enhances disorientation and confusion. It is unkind.

But it is also fascinating to blend these cultures and histories together in an uneasy, unplanned alliance. James Herren continues to be a Yankee fan, just as he was long before that very special day at the ballpark that he remembers so well: Lou Gehrig Day. Sam Poverelli uses his natural grammar to precisely articulate the difference between traditional Italian government and the Mussolini cult of personality. Then the sound of a beer glass punctuates the contrast between a sleepy Italian village and the flashpoint for world war. A candy store communicates the mood of the country at the end of WW II. Terrorism at the Curb Exchange shares its thoughts at the American Tomb of the Unknown Soldier. An immigrant's memory of an apple cake, described with Haiku-like elegance, remains cooling in memory for sixty years.

In these reflections you learn how to eat for free from an old Horn & Hardart, deliver Western Union telegrams, go fishing in Queens, make moonshine, remember Stella Dallas and achieve psychological insights into memory by touring Northern India with Socrates! The social history living in these rooms remains largely unrecognized by staff, by visitors, by residents who notice only that someone else has a better wheelchair or gets more attention — even by patients in the very same room!

This is the Last Call of a diverse New York immigrant population too stubborn to die, too hard working to quit, and too much a part of the swirling New York culture ever to leave. Often they are being cared for by a nursing staff composed of a new wave of immigrants who speak yet another tongue and enjoy different customs from any of the previous immigrants.

Many of the residents' children, grandchildren, and great-grandchildren write and visit from California, Illinois, North Carolina, and Florida. Others only went as far as Long Island or New Jersey. Many stayed on living in Italian, Irish, Jewish, Jamaican, and Greek enclaves somewhere within the "City." These immigrants lived through World Wars and several World Series'; they enjoyed the jazz age and remember when the Japanese invaded their China; they survive to live in small, usually bare-walled hospital-like rooms with roommates and staff who still speak with accents unlike their own.

Benny's Favorite Shoes
by Inez Johnson
(b. 1910; composed 1995)

I kept house
  For Benny Goodman's mother.
She sent Benny's shoes
  To a relative in Chicago.

But they were
  Benny's favorite shoes.
So she made me write a letter
  Asking for them back!

Eugene was in high school.
  Harry played in the band.
And the other one must've
  Been in grade school.

These jobs...
  They didn't
Pay you very much.
  You moved along...

Lou Gehrig Day
by James Herren
(b. 1906; composed 1995)

Whoa! It was a beautiful day!
80,000 people there hollering
"We want Lou!"
"We want Lou!"

All the players
Liked him on the team.
He played hard!
He played very hard!

He came from Columbia College
He went straight from college to Yankee Stadium
And he was well built — a good looking guy.
Never had a harsh word...for anybody.

That disease — it killed him.
People were going crazy,
They didn't know he was going to die.
It eats you away...that disease.

They had other ballplayers, too
But there will never be another
Lou Gehrig.
Never.

The Curb Exchange
by Steve Galligan
(b. 1902; composed 1996)

When the American Stock Exchange was the Curb Exchange
Located on Broad Street at Exchange Place
Men used to sit in windows and signal out to the curb
What to buy and what to sell.

You could walk along the street and see it —
There was no traffic allowed on Broad at that time.
Then around 1918 there was a Wall Street explosion —
I mean a real bomb explosion at the New York Stock Exchange.

A horse drawn truck was parked on Wall Street
Right in front of the Sub-Treasury Building.
(There are still marks on the building).
The horse was blown in half — split right open!

The force was so bad
Windowpanes came crashing down
Right into the Street.

I saw two men
With panes of glass
Sticking in their heads.

I saw women
Using their petticoats
For bandages.

The Curb Exchange stopped.
New York stopped.
The whole world stopped.

Our Candy Store
by Josie Brucaliere
(b. 1918; composed 1996)

We opened up in September, 1945.
The War had just ended
And they didn't need me
To make Eisenhower jackets anymore.

The candy store was on 2nd Avenue
Between 101st and 102nd streets
But more towards 101st
About 2 stores in from the corner.

All the men were coming home from the War
And the boys passed the word
That Joe and Josie Brooks
Had a candy store.

They came in,
Cashed their mustering out checks
(Those that hadn't died),
And started spending their money.

We put in a counter —
A soda fountain
On one side
Candy on the other.

18 cents for a malted milk.
3 cents for a plain chocolate soda.
5 cents for a big one.
A little more with a scoop of ice cream.

There were days...
A kid came in with no money
And a certain look on his face:
No charge for a soda!

The Best Shows
by Mary LaRosa
(b. 1913; composed 1995)

Shows? Oh, yes!
During one of the Depressions
I saw all of the shows.
The Ziegfield Follies,
Fred Astaire...

And on the radio
I remember Stella Dallas.
Let me see...
She had a daughter...

...And she was looking through the window
At her own daughter getting married...
Maybe the daughter was ashamed of her.

I lived in the best years!
The best songwriters,
The best shows,
The best showmen:
Ethel Merman, Eddie Cantor, Al Jolsen, and
Irving Berlin writing the best songs!

I used to see him on 42nd street —
I mean really see him
With people all around him!
And only 50 cents a Saturday to see a picture.

My Younger Days as a Worker
by Anna Caracciolo
(b. 1923; composed 1996)

My first job was Western Union:
Delivering telegrams.
If I got a 2 cent tip, I'd say
"Keep it! You need it worse than me."
Sometimes I'd get a quarter,
Sometimes nothing.

Then I made costume jewelry:
At home and in the factory.
I liked it —
I made 18 dollars a week!
My Mom did the same thing at home:
Piece work.

I worked in the Horn & Hardart, too:
Picking up dishes.
My sister worked in the kitchen
Giving out food.
Whenever I needed food
I just went to my sister.

It was fun when I went to work:
I enjoyed what I did.
And I did good work.
Of course they'd fire you if you didn't.
And a pink slip, with nothing on it, meant:
"Don't come back tomorrow."

In Queens, When it Rained, in 1926
by Edith Carr
(b. 1911; composed 1995)

In Queens, when it rained,
The streets were muddy.
We had cesspools you see, no sewers.

In Queens, when it rained,
We had to take our shoes off
Just to go in the house.

There was a lake on the corner
With swans and a hut for ice cream.
There were fish in the lake, too,

All in Queens.

BIG Shot
by Emmanuel Woodson
(b. 1917; composed 1995)

I never been in jail in my life.

The officers'll creep down on you
Right when you're working that still!

Chase me?
Yeah, they chase me.
But they don't know
If I got a gun or not!

You gotta be working
For a BIG shot,
For the BIG man.
Not some small shot.

You don't wanna work for nobody
Poorer than you is!
They can't do nothing for you
If you get in jail!

I didn't WANT to be a big shot.
I WAS one.

I Wonder Who He Was?
by Steve Galligan
(b. 1902; composed 1995)

The first year I worked
Right out of high school
I worked on Wall Street: 100 Broadway.

You can look right over Trinity Churchyard
And see the big boats with the soldiers
Sailing off the Europe on the Hudson River.

At the end of the war I was only sixteen years old
And they had a big parade down Broadway
Ending at City Hall, welcoming them back.

A fella by the name of Trinker,
A cashier in the firm I worked for,
My boss threw him a party when he went away.

But he didn't get his job back when he came home.
We had blackouts, with sirens,
And people in the streets making sure the lights were out.

I was too young to realize how many people died.
It was the Moms and Dads:
Their kids were buried in France.

When I was 17 I joined the National Guard
And stood guard over the unknown soldier:
I wonder who he was.

Could be a big shot.
Could be a pauper.
But, to us, he was hero.

Cella San Vito
by Stella Papa
(born 1896; composed, 1995)

A quiet town,
A plain town.
Nothing unusual,
But I loved it.

I want to be there now
Because it's plain:
Nothing fancy,
Easy to get along.

I feel like
It's my own town.

You could go.

Black Shirts
by Sam Poverelli
(b. 1909; composed 1996)

Black shirts.
Black ties.

It was two army.

One with the King.
One was Mussolini.

When the Beer Glass Hit the Table
by Louise Sprecher
(b. 1908; composed 1995)

"I was born under the French flag
and I'll always be French,"
my Dad would say.

I remember the name of the town:
Ingwiller, in Alsace.
(I just remembered it, while Hilda was talking).

The Germans wanted him in their army
And he wanted to come to America,
So he stopped in a saloon for a beer.

And he asked where France was.
"You're in Germany now," the bar keep said.
"France is right over there."

"Bang!" went the beer without even a sip.
My father went to France
To come to America.

It was his favorite story,
And I can always hear
The sound of that beer glass hitting the table

And see my father
Running out the door
To America.

Northern India
by George Socrates
(b. 1906; composed 1995)

I've been in Northern India: In Kashmir,
Where they travel by boat from house to house in Srinagar.

I worry about lots of things, even though I have a little money,
I don't want to need the government; That's why I work all my
life.

I'm not healthy, I know that.
My body...is not 100%.

Before you reach Kashmir is a place called Rawalpindi.
There's no trains —

And then you go to Srinagar
Which separates Pakistan from India.

I don't know myself how I remember all that!
Really, after all these years...I had forgotten about that.

In Gulmarg we went to sell embroidery:
I was a young fellow — very young

And my first sale was to the Maharajah of Kashmir.
I took a room in a boarding house and his was the first sale:

He was living in a temporary palace —
It was a Hindu place.

I'm glad how I remember — I guess I never forgot!
Once they knew the Maharajah bought, they all bought!

There's places all built in my mind
And I cannot forget.

We Were All Scared
Anonymous

I was scared...

When the Japanese
Were coming into
Canton Province.

And the people
Were not united,
Not united at all.

I cannot imagine
How this could have been...
I was such a little boy.

My father was sending us money
But we didn't always get it.
It was 1912 or something,

And we were all scared.

When I Left Ireland
by Sarah Fitzgerald
(b. 1926; composed 1996)

The last picture in my mind is
My mother baking an apple cake.

I saw it rise
When she checked it
In the oven.

She knew it was ready;
I don't know how
She knew it was ready.
She just knew.

I was a little hungry.
She cooled it on the table
And it just sat there

Apple cake
Alone
On the table.

Feminism

They don't call themselves feminists but the emotional seeds of a full blown movement are definitely scattering, finding soil and taking root in these expressive memory/poems. Finding a way to overcome what was sometimes a very oppressive male domination is a persistent theme of these surviving wives and mothers. To be sure, poems in other sections make clear that misbehaving fathers had disastrous effects on sons as well as on daughters. But when Bertha Hickey says "No Thank You," her tone of voice represents one woman's brave act of defiance.

The seeds of feminism are well watered in Elisa Pisani's memory "It Was Sort of Unfair!" and almost bloom when an anonymous author asks a very simple question: "How Come?" Catherine Kondel inadvertently suggests that Hell's Kitchen might have been a good place for feminism to take root, but Mary Cecco and Anna Payne both seem to reach a similar conclusion about the difficulties of life in this garden while the seeds are growing. "They Changed the Rules" is an understandable complaint considering the changes in religion and women's social roles between 1910 and 1996.

But the depth of emotional power circulating amidst these changes is best captured by Anna Schneider's remarkable insight, "God Has the Same Problem as the Wife." Like all good poetry, Anna's expression becomes more insightful and provocative over time. Her words are like the feminism blooming a little widly in these gardens we often think of as "rest homes."

No Thank You
by Bertha Hickey
(b. 1924; composed 1996)

This real good looking guy
Eyed me up and down
And then he decided to ask me to dance.
And that just got to me.

So I stepped back,
Eyed him up and down,
Walked around him, in fact,
And said, "No thank you."

It Was Sort of Unfair
by Elisa Pisani
(b. 1913; composed 1995)

It's easier for boys
To disobey their parents
Than for girls.
And my brother was one of them.

It must be more unfair
For girls than for boys.
It was more unfair for me
Than for my brother.

My Mother said:
"Don't you go out with that boy!" — a neighbor.
She had a premonition, maybe,
He wasn't going to wait for me.

Then one day
I opened the paper
And I saw his picture
On the wedding page.

I said "Who cares?"
It was my mother who stopped us.
He was handsome
And a nice boy.

I guess it wasn't meant to be.
I said "Forget it."
So I did.
But it was sort of unfair.

How Come?
Anonymous

Ever since I got older
I had more brains
Than when I was a girl.

I didn't use my brains then
But now that I'm older
My brain is very busy.

I was brought up
Not to use my brains.
I was a quiet girl.

My husband liked me quiet, too.
He was the boss
But now I wonder:

How come,
When you're older,
You get brainy?

And She Learned...
by Steve Galligan
(b. 1902; composed 1996)

My old man used to say
    "The road to Hell is paved with good intentions."
I used to ask him,
    "How would you know? You never had any."

It's a funny thing
    About my old man:
His father chased him out of the house
    And I chased him out of the house.

One day I was sitting in the living room
    And he started abusing my mother
I said: "Stop that!
    My mother is not a slave and she is not a hired hand."

After I chased him out of the house
    I felt...just natural.
My mother wouldn't stand up and argue.
    She took that abuse.

But I didn't want to and I didn't have to.

My old man...
    You couldn't eat an apple.
You couldn't rustle the newspaper.
    Because the noise would annoy him.

My Mom liked it when I stood up for her.
    So did my brother and my sister.
My Mom never did learn to stand up for herself.
    But my sister loved her mother

And she learned...

I Can Only Go To Heaven
by Catherine Kondel
(b. 1922; composed 1995)

When we were out looking for jobs
My Mom would say:
"Speak up! Or the person behind you
Will get the job!"

When we were traveling the subways
My father would say:
"If a man gets fresh with you,
Give him the elbow right in the gut."

I come from a rough neighborhood,
What they call "Hell's Kitchen" (39th to 59th).
So when I die, I can't go to Hell:
I can only go to Heaven.

Who Has It Better?
by Mary Cecco
(b. 1913; composed 1996)

Sometimes I think:
Who has it better —
A man or a woman?

It's six of one,
Five of another.
That's what I think!

Hurrah for the Boys!
Anonymous

The boys have the better deal.
I often wished I was one
Because they have it all over the woman.
She has no chance.

Men can just go into a corner,
Take a book out and read!
A woman's work is never done! Very satisfying...
But a man's got it all over a woman.

Just analyze it!
Just think about it!
You'll agree:
The boys have the better deal.

Even from the start up,
They're more watched over.
It's always: "Take care of Johnny now"--
Never: "Johnny, take care of your sister."

A woman has unpleasant things attached to her life
But the man gets the better deal.
If I had my gender to go by
I'd say "Hurrah for the boys!"

They Changed the Rules!
Anonymous

They changed the rules!
Women giving Communion?!
I don't even know
When they changed the rules!

Except for a few rules I disagreed with
I like they way I was brought up.
Maybe I'm really a Protestant...
Who the hell knows?

God Has the Same Problem as the Wife
by Anna Schneider
(b. 1904; composed 1996)

God doesn't know what to do
To please everybody.

Just like being married:
You try to please your husband and your children.

But somebody has to be hurt in life
And I think it is usually the wife.

She has to swallow most things
Or fight.

God has the same problem as the wife:
Trying to keep peace in the family.

Nursing Home Life

A nursing home is a commune without the idealism. Visitors and neighbors intrude on your dressing, your laundry may get lost until you spy it on someone else and others make decisions about what you eat, when you will eat it, and where you will sit. Your toileting habits become public knowledge and someone is sure to yell at you if you snore. The "old timers" who have been around for a few years tend to deny you favored spots to sit until you have been around long enough have "paid your dues." Just imagine being 85 years old and having to start "paying your dues" to enjoy such small bits of privilege!

Hilda Muller provides a glimpse into nursing home life with fellow residents as she describes her feelings about "The Street Walkers!" — a term she created to describe nursing home residents who wander, usually as the result of Alzheimer's disease or some variation of an organic brain syndrome. The particular wanderer she is describing became known among some of the residents as "Wandering Mary" and she moves so quietly she could have lived in a cloister: she drifts about almost silently, softly muttering to herself, and appearing to search for objects she desires but never can find. Consequently, she has the unnerving habit of drifting into residents' rooms, picking up favored items, and redepositing them at various points around the nursing home. (One of my first clues to nursing home creativity was the many different schemes residents came up with to keep "Wandering Mary" out of their rooms.) She also has incredible energy. On different occasions I have entered that particular nursing home at five in the morning, left late at night, and visited at odd hours; "Wandering Mary" was always awake and moving about with interest. It is curious how Hilda Muller comes to regard even this particularly irksome "Street Walker" with affection. It reminds us of the "Home" in Nursing Home and that Robert Frost described home as "the place where they have to take you in."

Another insight into nursing home life is provided by one resident's surprising reaction to her floormate. All day long they were seated about twelve feet apart and facing one another in their respective wheelchairs! The venom in the woman's tone of voice, her choice of language and the constancy of her hate were remarkable in themselves. It was a personalized hatred, actually fascinating in its energy and inventiveness. I remember hearing her say "You're disgusting...repulsive...we all want you to go away! You smell! You're unpleasant! Nobody likes you!" If it were possible to be meaner to this man, I don't know how a person would accomplish it. Three weeks after he died, the woman initiated the touching poem "That Corner is So Empty Now" as she reflected on his death.

In a nursing home people die so frequently that the long term survivors become understandably cautious about attachments. Hearing and sight difficulties also reduce the awareness of seatmates. Memory lapses are embarrassing and make relationships difficult to develop. Yet in spite of these deficits friendships still form, alliances continually shift, and reputations wax and wane. Catherine Kondel explains why she is a "fighter" for her aphasic roommate. An anonymous contributor pleads for "A Little Bit of Manners." In the context of this commune, the quality of friendship is both fleeting and generous.

Relationships with staff provide a different kind of insight into nursing home life. It is easy to resent staff, even when they practice their job with great sensitivity, because they hold such enormous power over nursing home residents' lives. Over time and innumerable personal situations, they may prove to be kind or brutal or a little bit of both. But they are the ones who change your bedding, provide necessary medications, offer rehabilitation, and have the power to stop by the drug store for a favorite candy bar, bottle of liquor, or preferred texture of tissues. There is an understandably high sensitivity to how such power is used. Mary Cecco expresses her anger and its justification clearly and passionately. The author of "A Lot of Trouble" indicates a some-times justified fear of retribution. The effort to be understand-ing of an overworked staff is poignantly expressed in "Pain, Pain" but reconsidered with perceptive honesty by the author of "Touchy...But They Call It Honest."

All of these expressions have in common a sense of lost control of the details of their own lives. Residents cannot con-trol the busy nursing staff who care for them; they cannot con-trol the doctors who don't like difficult cases; Margaret Ray ob-serves that she cannot even control the sounds of the nursing home which contrast so harshly with the predictable, friendly sounds of Irish farm life. A significant part of a psychological practice in a nursing home is assisting residents in how to use the power of their words to influence staff, and in learning which battles are worth fighting.

While it is easy for staff to engage in subtle (and even overt) brutality, many people working in nursing homes pos-sess an intuitive understanding of how important a sense of con-trol is to residents. I have observed nurses work so gently with residents, so compassionately careful in something as simple as administering multiple pills, that I want to cheer for humanity! On the other hand I have noted the sullen resentment of a poorly paid aide let loose on an annoying patient.

Families need to be vigilant, most staff deserve more train-ing and better pay, and nursing homes need to self-discipline — if they wish to establish and maintain standards of "Care." Unfor-tunately, not every nursing home does make a priority of qual-ity care. As you will see, much of the poetry in this section floats to the surface as a result of desperate nursing home cir-cumstances, both real and imagined.

As Ann Fulton points out, it is in our long term self-inter-est to improve the quality of care at nursing homes. She was a practicing poet long before we met. I am deeply concerned that her plea will need to linger on, long after we both have gone.

The Street Walkers!
by Hilda Muller
(b. 1911; composed 1995)

The street walkers
Creep into the rooms.
We're sleeping,
And then, suddenly,
There's someone there!

You jump together
You're so scared!
They're not supposed to do that!

Then you chase 'em...
They run like a weasel.
They don't sleep nights.

Those street walkers!

I Miss the Person
by Hilda Muller
(b. 1911; composed 1995)

I'm up, too, since six o'clock.
I sit in the chair in my room.
There's nobody here in the morning.
It's very quiet.

It's too quiet.
There's nobody here.
Fanny is gone for two weeks now,
And the Streetwalker is in the hospital.

At 6 o'clock, she used to walk up and down.
I miss the person; she was always a little excitement.
It was something to do to watch her.
She used to take her shirt off if she could.

I didn't like her,
But I miss her.
You live with them,
So you miss them.

How she could do it is what I wonder?!
From 6 in the morning until 8, 9 at night!
How many miles she did in a day!
I miss her; I miss the person.

Leave the Old Lady Alone!
by Hilda Muller
(b. 1911; composed 1995)

Oh, no! Fanny had a foot operation!
She won't be able to dance anymore.
I told her she shouldn't be getting in people's way.

The floor walker is back, though.
The one who runs like crazy:
She's still the same.

She grabs the old lady next to me.
She twists her napkin all up.
She did it yesterday and I hollered on her.

She is sick — I know about it.
I wouldn't shake hands with her, not for nothing.
You never know where those hands have been!

Leave the old lady alone!
She's 95 or 94 or 95; I'm not sure.
But the streetwalker wouldn't listen.

That Corner is So Empty Now
Anonymous

You know I miss him a little:
That man who died.
It's nice to have company talking to you.

Whatever he said doesn't mean a thing:
I think he hated everybody by the end;
He knew he was going to die.

I miss his talking.
He was so disgusted with everything.
That corner is so empty now.

Gossip
by Annie

Just to keep yourself busy;
You gossip.

You're bored;
You gossip.

You want to know things;
So you talk.

Not much happens here
So we have to talk all about it.

Injustice
by Catherine Kondel
(b. 1922; composed 1995)

We were coming out for lunch at 12 o'clock
When Philip Rizzo knocked my friend Mary down —
And her dress went up.
When the other boys seen her underwear,
They all had a good laugh.

When I was beating him up,
Along came the principal
And grabbed me and Philip by the shoulder
And took us to our classroom
And told my teacher: "A 'D' in conduct."

So I wasn't skipped:
  I had A,A,A,A,D.

But I'm named after St. Catherine of Padua:
  a fighter.
I'm descended from Romans, Vikings, and the Irish:
  all fighters.
So I was always looking out for the other man.

I fought for a railing for my roommate:
  She was going to break her neck.
I won this one:
  My prayers were answered.

A Little Bit of Manners
Anonymous

Because you're older
Don't mean you have to be pushy.

You could show
Just a little bit of your manners.

A Lot of Trouble
Anonymous

If I had to do it again
I wouldn't do it.
Because I got in a lot of trouble.

They say patients have a right to speak up
But they don't.
Because they get in a lot of trouble.

You can publish this, of course.
Just don't put my name on it.
Because I would get in a lot of trouble.

Pain, Pain
by Sam Poverelli
(b. 1909; composed 1995)

Pain, pain
I can't move my bowels
I can't make pee-pee.

I told the nurse
But they're busy
Right now.

Vacant Spots
by Anna Schoeps
(b. 1914; composed 1996)

I read...
To fill in the vacant spots.

I read...
To pass the time.

I read...
About other people's experiences.

I find...
That I missed a lot.

Touchy...But They Call It Honest
by Bertha Hickey
(B. 1924; composed 1996)

There are days when I'm not honest
Then, when I get myself together
I say, "You can't judge other people
For the way you sometimes are."

It's not good to be touchy, either.
It's better to roll with the punches.
If you don't learn this,
You'll be hurt all your life.

And it will change your personality!
Some people here are touchy —
They're touchy...but they call it honest.
It's not the same thing.

I guess it makes them feel good,
As if they're up on a pedestal
When they force people to eat
Just to show how concerned they are.

Doctors
by Doris Marshall
(b. 1917; composed 1996)

Doctors don't like a difficult case.
I know I'm going to die anyway,
But they won't tell me that.
They won't admit it, I guess,
That they don't know the answer.

Maybe there is no answer.
I've been a difficult case
And sometimes I think
They don't like me.
Maybe I make them feel uncomfortable.

I'd Like to Choose It
by Jane Hodik
(b. 1901; composed 1996)

I wouldn't like a rest home.
I would have no choice.

If I have a choice,
I'd like to choose it.

Sounds
by Margaret Ray
(b. 1903; composed 1996)

I miss hearing the cows moo-ing.
When it's time to get milked
They let you know it's time.

And the chickens begin to squawk
When they lay an egg.
They let you know that it's there.

A storm was a bad sound:
The wind sounded like it could
Knock over one of the old oaks onto the house.

Once a storm lasted all night long — It was Really Scary!
There were a lot of sheep high on the mountain
Killed with the lightening; the wind went through with a rush.

Living here
The sounds are terrible, like thunder:
But they never go away.

I ask them but they say they don't know
What makes all those sounds.
It's continual, never stops, always a bother.

You have to go through.
It never goes away.
And there's nothing you can do.

Be Kind
by Ann Fulton
(b. 1913; composed 1996)

Be kind to the people that are placed in your care,
Someday you, yourself, may also be there

They are in their old age, through no fault of their own,
They are in a position where their needs have grown,

For love and understanding, and sympathy, too
May you have patience to what they may do.

They may cause your temper to flare up and rise,
Just remember, that someday you may utter those cries.

That you have heard the people, that need understanding, then,
You'll do your best to make them smile again.

Anger and Depression

The words presented in this section are not trivial, yet they are offered so casually that I feel like a wine connoisseur invited to taste from a newly discovered cellar just before the roof caves in. Even when triggered by some minor nursing home event, these are expressions of a mature anger and a seasoned depression, some of which have aged in the cool quiet of their psyches for eighty and ninety years.

Many nursing home residents have been prepared to die for several years and they have become both angry and depressed in the waiting. Others see their entrance into a nursing home as the last stop to the destination of death and become depressed when they realize that they continue to live. The author of "But What For?" knows how to live cheerfully, lives cheerfully most of the time, yet still he prefers to die! These poems are refined expressions of raw emotions.

But anger and depression do not need to be chronic states among most nursing home residents. Present experience re-engages past cognitions, which is a somewhat academic way of pointing out the obvious: if our present situation is depressing, it makes it easier for us to remember previous depressions. On the other hand, if our current situation is encouraging, then we recall other periods of hopefulness and fulfillment.

In one study, we simulated the nursing home experience among healthy college students. We limited their physical function, general mobility, and speech. We surrounded them with peers imitating an Alzheimer patient, other dementias, and some physical dysfunctions such as arthritis in the hands and lack of mobility. The students displayed depressive symptoms and reported a dramatic lowering in their sense of control. For nursing home residents, what happens in the here and now also makes a tremendous difference in their quality of life.

The two poems entitled "Today" and "Like Digging a Hole in My Grave" refer to how those individuals were experiencing life in the nursing home. Their present experience nurtures their depressive potential. But research has already clarified both techniques and underlying principles which easily and dramatically enhance the quality of life among nursing home residents (see especially work by Ellen Langer and Judith Rodin, briefly summarized in *Forty Studies That Changed Psychology* by Roger Hock). Just as a negative present reminds residents of negative features of their past, a positive present also will help to re-engage positive habits and capabilities.

Prevalence rates for depressive disorders range from 10% to as high as 60%, depending on criteria (Hay et al., 1996, *Nursing Home Medicine*, 4, 4, 104-109). But such research often assumes that the cause (and subsequent treatment) of depression is organic and physiological rather than situational and psychological. The cause of widespread nursing home depression is <u>both</u> physiological and situational. If we can create significant levels of depression among healthy college students in a half hour simulation, then how much more powerful is the actual uninterrupted nursing home situation at causing depression among a population with genuine physical and mental deficits! Our current (often justified) fascination with psychotropic interventions should not serve as an excuse for neglecting the sublime benefits of human contact — a diagnosis of probable Alzheimer's Disease or Organic Brain Syndrome does not justify abandonment by family members!

This book asserts, as powerfully as I can demonstrate it, that people in nursing homes are capable of far more wisdom, insight, pleasure, and expression than our stereotype allows us to believe. If we look for creativity, we will discover it; if we anticipate dementia, we will help produce it!

Broken
by Anna Schneider
(b. 1904; composed 1995)

I'm all broken up:
Broken tooth. See!
Broken leg. See!
From top to bottom: I'm broken.
I can't even think, I'm so broken.

Something I didn't expect — ever:
Falling to pieces.

Well, that's the way it goes.

Angry
Anonymous

When I'm angry...
My mouth just flows.

Angry Because
Anonymous

...that they don't let me do as I want!
I get instructions: "Do this!" "Don't do that!"
Right now I'm not even wearing a goddamn bra!
And you know that's important for a woman!
It's probably on someone else!

...that they don't give me 2 cents!
They don't give a damn!
And they keep their ears open
To anything anybody says!
And I never even get my own checks!

That's why I'm angry!

Depressed?
by Anna Caracciolo
(b. 1923; composed 1996)

No, I don't get depressed.
If I do,
I don't remember.

No, I don't get anxious either.
Once or twice a long time ago
But that was enough.

I'm not angry too often either.
I hold it in for a while
And then I forget about it.

The only time I got depressed
Was when my Mother died.
Or was it my Father?

But What For?
Anonymous

Everyday I get up
I wonder if I'm going to get through it.

But I'm not afraid —
It has to happen someday.

It don't cost me nothing to live cheerful.
But what for?

The Women Here
Anonymous

The women here...
Sometimes they're so confusing.
Sometimes they play jokes.
There's more women than men.

The women here...
We have not much to do with the women.
I don't like to talk to them.
There are always two or three together at a time.

The women here...
They make jokes and I don't know what they're about.
I'm all alone here.
I'm all alone in my family.

Loneliness
by George Socrates
(b. 1906; composed 1996)

You never get used to it.
You just go along with it.

Loneliness.

I've been lonely
For many years.

She Has a Doll
Anonymous

It's not easy when you have very little family.
Not one bit.

My daughter was supposed to be here.
My son-in-law was supposed to be here.

I feel let down:
They were supposed to be here.

I don't know how I stand it.
I wonder where we got these rules from?

It was a rule.
They were supposed to be here.

But there's a woman here
Who has just a doll.

No rules, no daughter, no son-in-law —
Nobody at all as far as I can tell.

But she has a lot more than I have:
She has a doll.

Today
Anonymous

Today.
I hope today
Is my last day
Here.

This Is Not My Style!
Anonymous

This is not my style.
This living is not living.

Friends
by Stella Papa
(b. 1896; composed 1995)

In the beginning, here,
I had two friends.
Then they all went away.

Now I haven't got.
No one to tell things to.
I haven't got any more friends.

Excuse My Language, but...
Anonymous

I'd like to take and strip them
Right in front of everybody
And then see how they'd feel!

I just scream
And drop everything
And throw it over me!

Excuse my language
But shit, shit, shit!
I'd like to throw it right in their face!

Like Digging a Hole in My Grave
Anonymous

This here is like
Digging a hole in my grave.
I would just as soon
Be done with it.

Tired of Living
by Elisa Pisani
(b. 1913; composed 1995)

I'm such a dumbbell: I fell.
I'm surprised to see
I am so yellow.

Tell you the truth:
I'm tired of living.
Tired of all this nonsense.

Tired of me.

Feelings

I have feelings...
  That others
Don't have feelings
  Towards me.

Now I Want to Disappear
Anonymous

I don't want to pray anymore
I don't care anymore.
I just want to close the door.
Close the door inside my apartment.

We saved $1,000.00 a year
Every year for forty years.
At the end of this month
Every single penny will be gone.

Everything is disappeared.
Now I want to disappear.

I paid everything:
Every promise,
Every bill,
Every time,
Every one.

Blue Cross,
Blue Shield,
Medicaid,
Medicare,
Every doctor.

One operation.
One month.
All gone.

How Lonely I Am!

by Bertha Hickey
(b. 1924; composed 1996)

I'm angry because of my situation
I'm angry because my situation
Is beyond my control.

I can't do
What I want to do
When I want to do it!

For example,
People don't understand me.
I'm not that far out or different!

For example,
When they call me "She"
Instead of my name!

For example,
When nobody calls me,
Not friends or family

Then I think "I'll get even!"
I know it's wrong
But I can't help it.

I'm supposed
To understand
How busy they are!

They're supposed
To understand
How lonely I am!

Marriage and Families

For several months, a quiet and dignified elderly gentleman entered the nursing home at 9:30 AM and sat downstairs waiting for visiting hours to begin. Every day. At 10 AM, he entered the elevator and when the doors slid open again, his wife would greet him with a brilliant smile, a smile with such pleasure in it that I would wait around the nurses' station just to see it, and feel the loving challenge to my own marriage. Then they would sit, holding hands like teenagers, reading the newspaper, and chatting about one thing or another. Then it would be time to go. Eventually, he too needed nursing home care. He obtained a room on a different floor. And now, every morning, he takes the elevator downstairs to the lobby at 9:30, reenters the elevator half an hour later, and repeats the ritual that is so satisfying to the woman he loves.

A quiet point and counterpoint pattern alternates throughout these poems about marriage, families, children and parents. In their memories, residents are coping with parental strictness on the one hand ("Strict" and "I Did What I Want") and enduring affection on the other ("We Never Went Out for Lunch" and "We'll Go Fishing, Me and You"). The pain of absent or abusive fathers is carried across eighty years by Steve Galligan but gives way to marriage and dedication in Sam Poverelli's recollections "I Remember the Day" and "I Give Myself Credit." What powerful fathers live in these memories, for good and ill.

Questions about marriage and children seem to elicit humor, sentimentality and a sweet sense of romance among many of these contributors. Most of the residents, I think, tend to hide the pain of poor marriages. One resident, however, continues to plead plaintively for more understanding from her husband, his physical absence no deterrent to her determination to persuade. Alice Mishkin's succinct, telling definition of "Marriage" receives some elaboration by Sal Giglio who was responding to my deliberately naive question of whether he and his wife had ever argued. Ibrahim Chowdry offers some advice that feels hard won, accurate, and practical.

Children, of course, are a significant part of the memories that exist between couples and Sam Poverelli's dramatic words attest to the enduring place children hold in their parents' minds. But among the words offered here I sense a greater focus on the marriage than on the children. Margaret Ray's memory of first love survived even the man who inspired it. Catherine Kondel's husband was the chief object of her semi-serious plea "Give Me the Money." It is pride in her husband that inspires Anna's poem "Brooks Brothers." Finally, Emmanuel Woodson seemed to capture something poignantly true about how children grow up and away from their parents. Perhaps this is why parents seem to occupy such a large place in nursing home residents' thoughts: children usually live on but move away; parents only live on in memories that seem impossible to destroy.

🐾

Marriage
by Alice Mishkin
(b. 1911; composed 1995)

Marriage:
The one time in life
You never get over.

I Remember the Day
by Sam Poverelli
(b. 1909; composed 1996)

I met my wife when she was born:
She was neighbor on a farm.

I like like a friend
Then I like like a lover.

She's the only woman I know.
I am the only man she know.

Every night on the farm there was a dance.
One night this house and another night that house.

When I was 17 I had to go in the army.
I thought "Someone will take my wife, my beautiful girlfriend."

So I asked my father,
"I love this girl — I want to get married."

He say: "You really love her?
You can support her?"

He said "Yes. Get married."
I remember the day.

Then they dropped a bomb and killed him.
I would have married her no matter what he said.

Sam
by Margaret Ray
(b. 1903; composed 1996)

He used to work in Grand Central Station:
Assistant Baggage Master, he was.
He had 500 men under him
And he was good to every one of them.
He was the best in the world.

We met at a dance.
(It's a good story,
And it's a true one...
I'm Irish, you know.)

It was love at first sight.
He was wearing a gray suit.
The next thing
He wanted to dance with me
And that was it —
Nobody could come between us!

Adjust Yourself — Continuously
by Ibrahim Chowdry
(b. 1906; composed 1996)

Many people ask me about marriage.
Unless you are very good at understanding
You better keep away.

You'll be very unhappy in life
If you have to fight with your wife,
So adjust yourself.

You can't adjust someone else...
It's very hard...very hard indeed...
It's best if both adjust themselves.

You have to adjust yourself
To be happy in life —
Continuously.

We Never Had a Problem
A Little Ice Cream Couldn't Fix
by Sal Giglio
(b. 1912; composed 1996)

I won't say we didn't argue....
We were married for fifty-seven years
And kept company for three years before that.

But I tell you what I did:
She didn't like the chocolate and I didn't like the vanilla.
So she got the vanilla and I got the chocolate.

Nothing runs smooth — we all know that.
But we never had a problem
A little ice cream couldn't fix.

Brooks Brothers
by Anna

I saw a man who comes here
Who wears Brooks Brothers.
I said, "There goes Brooks Brothers!"
Most people don't know.

My husband wears Brooks Brothers —
Right down to his underwear!
It means money, you know.
He bought everything on special.

He's retired.
From Brooks Brothers.

I Give Myself Credit
by Sam Poverelli
(b. 1911; composed 1996)

I was scared. I said "Please, God!"
Then, when the stamp went down I felt wonderful!
I was in Cuba for just one day — asking me questions.
I don't speak Spanish — or English too good. I speak Italian.

I was in America for six years: I stow away on a ship,
But to become citizen, I go Cuba. After six years,
And then all of a sudden I'm a citizen! I go right up to a cop.
Right away I called my wife and my kids in Italy.

When the stamp went down I was so happy
Because the lawyer said "Hurry up!"
They got on the last boat out of Italy: The "Rex!"
They just made it, my family. I was so happy.

I give myself credit. Nobody else did, so I did.
The lawyer was a Jew on 42nd St. in NY: Sinkman.
Maybe he's still alive, but I don't think so.
He did a lot for me and for other people, too.

My mother-in-law came, too. My mother and my brother
And my other brother. And my two sons.
When I see my two boys after six years in America:
So happy I can't tell you!

They were six and nine years old!
When the "Rex" appeared at night at the dock,
My boys, my boys shouted "Hey, Papa! Hey, Papa!"
They recognized me from pictures! Thank God! Thank God!

Take It As It Comes
by Anna Schneider
(b. 1904; composed 1995)

Four girls?
You overdid it!

Whatever you get,
Just keep your mouth shut!

They've All Grown
by Emmanuel Woodson
(b. 1917; composed 1995)

No, I don't have any children.
They've all grown.

I Did What I Want
by Elisa Pisani
(b. 1913, composed 1995)

I disobeyed my Mom:
I went on a trip
With my old schoolteacher: Marie.

We went through Kentucky
(The grass is really blue),
Mississippi, Missouri.

Then we came back
Through Chicago,
Back home to New York.

It's hard to believe
That I took that trip —
That I disobeyed my Mom.

Just once, I did what I want.

We'll Go Fishing, Me and You
Anonymous

Who was my family?
I remember only my father.
Because once in a while
He would see me here.

But now I know he's died.

My father said,
"We'll go fishing, me and you.
Because pretty soon I'm going to retire.
We'll go fishing."

I remember only this:
I had a nice man
Who once in a while...
Go fishing...

We buy lunch before...
In a boat, we eat...
And we go fishing.
It was nice, really.

Strict
Anonymous

The Nuns were strict.
My father was strict.
He was good to us...
There's no sense in saying anything else.

My mother died when she was 35 years old.
I don't remember her very well:
She didn't have nothing to say over us.

But my father was strict —
Never gave us any money
To go to the movies
Or anything.
No friends to play with.
Very strict.

Naturally,
He thought he was doing
The right thing.

This is My Dad!
by Steve Galligan
(b. 1902; composed 1996)

When she was twenty-one
My Mother had three children
And then her husband died.

As a widow she ran the numbers
Picking them up from the firehouse:
My Father was a fireman.

He married my Mother
Because she wouldn't have sex
Without being married.

He was the lousiest S-O-B in the world:
Wouldn't support any of the children,
Called them "Consumptive Bastards!"

This is my Dad:
We lived on 52nd street
But he never took me to Central Park.

Once he took me to Rockaway on the train:
I'm seven years old
And he started flirting.

I said "That isn't my Mother!"
He didn't say nothing but he stopped:
She wasn't paying attention.

We had one vacation:
He brought his girlfriend
To the very same hotel.

Everyone thought
My Mother was a nursemaid:
This is my Dad.

We Never Went Out For Lunch
by Elise Brennan
(b. 1913; composed 1995)

I had lunch every day with my father
He would pick me up from the college: NYU.
We would go on...it was like a trolley car...
To a restaurant.

We went every day.
I often think about that.
I have two children: a boy and a girl.
And I understand that

My girl came to see me two days ago.
She said "We look alike, Mom."
But I never took her out for lunch.
There was never time for that.

But we used to laugh a lot,
Me and my daughter.
We went on vacations...
But we never went out for lunch.

Not a Sweet Eater
by Catherine Kondel
(b. 1922; composed 1995)

I told him all the time:
"Don't give the gift,
Give me the money!"

Like on Valentine's Day
I'd get a heart-shaped box of candy.
Give me the money!

The store clerks see a man,
And they'll take advantage of him.
Give me the money!

Keep it simple!
I'll go play BINGO!
Just give me the money!

Pop is Gone
by Sal Giglio
(b. 1912; composed 1996)

My father died in my arms.
He looked at me
And went away.

I told my sister,
"Pop is gone."
I miss him.

The whole family was there that night.
I said to them all,
"Pop is gone."

We all sat quietly.
Then I called the undertaker.
He said, "He's gone."

Curiosity

Perhaps nothing captures the mental and emotional struggles of nursing home residents as well as the recognition of their profound curiosity. Many are trying to puzzle out, along with the author of "What Happened?" how in the world they ever managed to end up dazed and confused in an "old age home." But the quality of curiosity is far richer than answering the question of how they arrived in a nursing home, especially among those who see death as an opportunity to get answers to some difficult questions. The poem "Some Day" was expressed with real confidence that answers would be forthcoming. The rich philosophy Esther Carroll articulates (after an admittedly rather bizarre beginning) is a deeply human affirmation that even our curiosity has a purpose, that there is a purpose even in hopelessness.

Margaret Ray adds the recognition that curiosity continues; the puzzle of dreams and how the brain produces such odd yet compelling combinations continues to intrigue her as much as it did when she was young. One of the few things I was able to discover about Rose Huber before she died was the recognition offered here that her curiosity for details remained constant across her entire life; even the memory of earlier mysteries remained a mystery. However, these nursing home residents are not uniformly passionate to discover something new about life. In fact, Elizabeth Sheridan quite eloquently explains why she restrains her own sense of wonder. But for the most part, these nursing home residents remain curious about themselves, about life and religion, about their own mental capabilities — even about curiosity!

What Happened...?
Anonymous

My memory...
I was, until,
I didn't know nothing...
Then, before Easter,
My son came to visit me,
And he said, "What happened?"

I didn't know what happened.
I knew I had no house.
I knew I had no family.
Hey! What happened to me?

I don't know.
I'm just here.

We were 3 people:
My sister and her husband and me
And a car accident.

Why? Don't they write to me?
Why? Don't they come to see me?

A beautiful house.
Furniture.
Why?

I want to know more how happened what happened.

I Can't Seem to Die
by Esther Carroll
(b. 1911; composed 1995)

I hope for an early death
Especially after what I've seen here.
Who wants to suffer, for God's sake?
  My coughing is back.
  My angina is back.
  My back hurts with my chest pain.
You take one medicine to fix one thing and
It makes something else worse than the first thing.
Pain and age and incapacitation...Who wants it?
  I think of all I've lost and
  How long it took me to accumulate it.
  I can't take it with me when I do die

And I will die...someday.

You don't get what you want in this life:
People who want to live a long time die young
And me? I can't seem to die.
  You live to learn.
  That's all I can figure.
  And I guess I haven't learned it yet.
And what it is I have no idea.
I thought I knew everything when I came here
But now I know better because I've learned a lot here.

And I Still Don't Know...
Anonymous

Some of my years I was scared.
Some of my years I was worried.

And I still don't know
How it's going to be.

I Just Can't Understand
By Doris Marshall
(b. 1917; composed 1996)

I just can't understand
Why nobody understands me.
They think they do,
But they don't.

Wouldn't it be interesting
If lots of other people
Felt the way I feel —
That nobody understands them?

Some Day
Anonymous

Some day,
I'll find out
All the whys
I've been wondering.

What Crazy Dreams!
by Margaret Ray
(b. 1903; composed 1995)

What crazy dreams!

I dreamed I was with my sister Betty —
But she's dead.

We were going to visit our cousins in Canada —
But they're dead.

What crazy dreams!

Something for Christmas
by Rose Huber
(b. 1913; composed 1995)

I'd pick it up
And shake it
And try to figure out
What was in it.

My Mom was watching me.
She'd say, "What are you doing?
Do you want to know what's in it?"
She'd say, "Something for Christmas."

I don't know why
I remember that so well.

I just do.

Sometimes I Wonder
Elizabeth Sheridan
(b. 1906; composed 1995)

Sometimes I wonder...
Am I really in charge of myself?

Don't think about it too much.
It might not be such a good idea.

Aging

The life patterns which make up the lives of these nursing home residents are not always clear — to themselves or to me. Most of them know they are getting old, yet they continue to respond to the old impulse to try and make sense out of their lives. Naturally, they are most aware of their own experience — an experience that includes odd details strewn across almost a century of living! In order to sneak a look at how these residents were seeing the pattern of their own lives as it arose from these details, I used a simple, pleasant sentence completion technique to get them started, prompting them with "When I was young...." and waiting while they filled in the blanks. Together, we began to perceive some patterns.

The life pattern that emerges from these details is wonderfully unique to each resident. Although her logic is a bit slippery, I somehow still follow Florence Robertson's experience in which she concludes that it would be nice to be rich. Aging might be a bit more pleasant with a bit more money. Every stage of life would have been a bit more pleasant with a bit more money. When Andreas Constantinou articulates what he finds "Most Important" he seems to be describing personal honesty, a pattern that permeates every one of his poems — I hope you have noticed. Madeline Vermilya's response started me writing down residents' words with an ear for their poetry. Her casual insight into the unity behind so much varied human experience caught my attention. The larger pattern formed by all these individual lives merging together in the difficult communal context of a nursing home is also starting to form, in spite of the wide individual differences in how people grow old.

The nursing home situation provokes personality change. Not dramatic change, necessarily, but the rock of personality continues to wear away, taking on unusual but distinctive shapes. One twenty-seven year old granddaughter described the introspection provoked by her grandmother's comment that she wished she hadn't been so sexually faithful to her husband in her younger years. Her grandmother's motivation seemed to be more curiosity than romantic disillusionment, but the family was certainly startled at the Grandmother's reflections. Several of the poems in other sections suggest things like "It's only lately that I'm beginning to think for myself," or ask "How come, when you get old, you get brainy?" Poems in this section also indicate that somehow life is very different at different stages and that life seldom worked out just the way they thought it would work out. Personality, beliefs, and attitudes all continue to change.

That people continue to change right up to the very end of their lives is not very startling. What I find more interesting is the relative purity of the emerging attitudes. Pretense, reputation and worry about what others are thinking all seem pretty pointless by the time you land in a nursing home. It is not just the fact of continuous personality adjustment that makes psychotherapy with this population so rewarding, it is the quality of that personality adjustment — the recognition that psychologically we are unlikely ever to be more clear eyed about life than we are right now. It is the freedom from convention, obligation and social pressure that can make aging so delightful in spite of its difficulties. The personal discoveries are relaxing even when they are a bit frightening. There seems to be a quietly bubbling spring of psychological mischievousness which many people living in nursing homes find especially enjoyable.

Just prior to publication, one resident came up to me and said "I've been thinking about my poem and I'm thinking maybe you shouldn't use my name when you publish it. My daughter might read it." I assured her, of course, that whatever she decided was fine with me. We chatted about that for a while and she changed her mind again. "Oh, let her read it," she said. "It's all true. And anyway...what the hell!"

Completely Forgetting to Keep Track of One's Age
by Sarah Fitzgerald
(b. 1926; composed 1996)

When I was young
I never thought of growing old.

When I was middle aged
I never give it a thought.

Now that I am older
I completely forgot about it.

Can You Beat That?
Anonymous

My youngest is 63.
My oldest is 68.
Can you beat that?

It Must Be Nice to be Rich
by Florence Robertson
(b. 1906; composed 1995)

All this scaly stuff on my face:
It must come from
Getting old...and feeble.
It must be nice to be rich!

When I Was Old
Anonymous

When I was young
    Life was hard.

When I was middle aged
    Everything came harder.

When I was old
    It began to get better.

Now I am 94 —
    I got nothing to worry about.

Most Important
by Andreas Constantinou
(b. 1907; composed 1996)

I was thinking yesterday
That the most important thing
Was to do this, that, and the other
And to be clear about it.

You don't try to make believe
That you forgot it.
You just try to be
The way you're supposed to be.

Last Licks
by James Herren
(b. 1906; composed 1996)

I'm 90 years old...
On my last licks,
Believe me.

You have to take
The bad with the good.
There's no way out.

The way I see it,
They're not playing together:
The owners and the players.

They don't want to give in,
Neither of them.
But baseball will go on forever.

Quotations From the Past
by Esther Carroll
(b. 1911; composed 1995)

Fifty years!
But I didn't lose it:
My Louisiana accent.
It was normal to me — still is.

Fifty years?
It sure went by quickly!
Don't know how,
But it did.

Fifty years...
A lot of things can happen.
You don't expect them,
But then you do the best you can.

I was born in Texas,
But I went to New Orleans
When I was three and a half —
So it's really my home town.

I've only been up North
For fifty years.

Young and Old
by Madeline Vermilya
(b. 1911; composed 1995)

When I was young
 I was foolish.
When I was young
 I was happy.
Same thing, isn't it?

When I was old
 I was crabby.
When I was old
 I was happy.

Same thing, Isn't it?

Stirring the Waters

This book demonstrates that many people who live in nursing homes are capable of diverse and sublime creativity. It is not a terribly deep message to assert that we can discover their creativity by providing nursing home residents with what many of the rest of us also want: attentive listening. "Attention must be paid" proclaims the wife of the aging Willie Loman in *Death of a Salesman*. But the unfortunate reality of life in American nursing homes is that attention does not have to be paid — and that frequently it is not paid. Futhermore, the desire to pay attention cannot be legislated into families, physicians, psychologists, or nurses. Training can help, of course, but only when listening becomes a pleasure rather than an obligation.

The therapeutic working out of "paying attention" to the frail elderly provides them with the balance between physical security and psychological control which supports the creativity demonstrated in this book. Unfortunately, nursing homes usually seek to provide security by taking away control. The two goals do not need to be in conflict. Just imagine how creative the elderly voices in your own family could be — if you will listen, carefully, to the words they are saying.

Some of the creativity represented in this book might not have taken shape without the life pressures which eventually created the need for a nursing home. Like a pool of hidden water gently lapping the rocks of an ancient cave, nursing home creativity is quietly waiting to be discovered, splashed in, tapped. It requires, usually, someone else to stir the waters because fatigue, disbelief, habit, and deafness conspire to keep people living in nursing homes away from the startling pool of their own creativity. But reading the words in this book should convince you: old rocks can hold living waters, and they have many things to tell you.

Tom Heinzen   October, 1996

About the Author

Dr. Heinzen received his Bachelor of Science in General Studies from Rockford College in Illinois and his Ph.D. in Social Psychology from the State University of New York at Albany. He is a clinically licensed psychologist, trained in cognitive therapy, who has conducted research in conjunction with the Johns Hopkins University Center for Talented Youth, the Professional Development Program in New York State at the Rockefeller College of Public Affairs and Policy, the New York Center for Agricultural Medicine and Health, and the Institute for Creative Aging at Wm. Paterson College in New Jersey. He has published numerous scientific articles in journals such as *Hospital and Community Psychiatry, Clinical Geriatrics, Public Productivity and Management Review, Roeper Review, Sex Roles, Creativity Research Journal, The American Journal of Distance Education, and Journal of Management Science and Policy Analysis.* He has also authored additional books individually *(Everyday Frustration and Creativity in Government, The Frustration-Creativity Hypothesis)* and contributed chapters to others *(Affect and Creativity and Creativity Processes).* He and his wife Donna are the parents of four daughters, Amy, Debbie, Elizabeth and Rebekah and currently live in Glen Ridge, New Jersey.